Life on Earth

PEGGY HALL FLAGG

Copyright © 2017 Peggy Hall Flagg

All rights reserved.

ISBN-13: 978-0692993170 (Silver Pegasus Publishing)
ISBN-10: 0692993177

DEDICATION

To all the people who love and respect Mother Earth.

The earth has its music for those who will listen.

- George Santayana

CONTENTS

	Acknowledgments	i
1	Life on Earth	1
2	Past Lives	5
3	Creation	7
4	Negativity	9
5	Energy	11
6	Medicines	13
7	Trees	15
8	Plants	19
9	Animals	25
10	The Next Step	29
11	The Rugged Landscapes That We Call Home	35

ACKNOWLEDGMENTS

I would like to thank my granddaughter Hannah Flagg for contributing the final chapter and her beautiful photographs to this book and Sinari Diliiza for her original illustrations.

LIFE ON EARTH

I want to share with you some of the things I have come to believe after forty years in the metaphysical world and my experiences which are numerous.

I became interested in the metaphysical field at an early age with an inner knowing that there must be much more to life than I could see or was experiencing. I starting searching and really didn't get any answers until I was around thirty three years of age. From then on my life centered around finding more meaning to life and what I came here to do. I was always involved in a program that offered self discovery and how to develop psychic ability where I found answers for myself and then could pass information along to others.

I believe that we come to earth to learn lessons and grow in awareness. We are not alone in this journey as we come with angels, teachers and guides to help us if we ask and listen to what they are saying. This is an agreement between them and us before we incarnate. They have already mastered what we came to do.

We come with a different number of helpers, depending on our mission this lifetime. If a person came to work with things then we have one or two helpers to give inspiration. If we came to work with people than we have three or more. We always have all the help we need as there are roving teams that come in to help us if needed. They usually are here about six months. An example of this is when I was in a program I was put in charge of promotion, which is not my favorite. I was an administrator but I was told when you get comfortable in one position you aren't growing any more. I asked angels for help and I had a large team move in to help me. They were with me until I was more comfortable in my position.

Do you communicate with your angels? If not, they are waiting for you to talk with them. They have been feeding you information for a long time. They protect you in many cases. They arrange things you may say are coincidental and when they come close to you, you may experience them as chills or a feeling of well being.

Sometimes my angels come to me to share some information they want me to know or information that I have asked for. Sometimes I talk to them in prayer or maybe ask for advice on something. Many times I have asked for direction. Before I would make what I call a big decision I would ask them for their opinion. For example, one winter I was going to Puerto Rico to take a one week course and there were four different courses each a week long so I asked my angels which week would be most beneficial for me to go. I went by what guidance suggested because I knew they saw a bigger picture than I. Another time there were six or eight of us out for dinner in New Mexico. I couldn't decide what I wanted to order so asked my angels what would be best for me and they told me so I ordered what they suggested. Three people in our group ordered a fish dinner with s cream sauce and that night and next morning they were sick with food poisoning.

To start communicating with angels (or sometimes I say Spirit because we have different souls we work with) always deep breathe and clear your mind of other things. I use different techniques to prepare for communication. The easy one I recommend is to see a white light surrounding yourself take a deep breath and ask Spirit to come close to you. Sometimes you may feel chills when they are around. Depending on what you want for communication is how you begin. If you want an answer to something then ask the question and listen. Or ask them if they can back you in some situation. It's just practice, practice until you feel you can trust what you hear.

There are also what I call little people here on earth that came to help. They are in a different dimension so not everyone sees them. There are elementals who do a lot of good cleaning up our messes. I love watching when they clean up the atmosphere. Their light ship emits a cloud like cover around them. If you see a lot of small individual clouds in the sky that's the elementals cleaning the atmosphere. They also work on purifying the water and land.

There are really fairies, sprites and gnomes. My husband had a relationship with a family of gnomes for a couple of years. He said they lived in the banking by the garden. He used to talk with them and they would help in the garden if they could have some food. They are an odd sect as they can be very loving and they can also be very possessive of things. My husband knew for sure that they helped weed the garden. At times he actually saw the gnomes. He would carry on a conversation with them, though sometimes he didn't know if he was really talking with them or he made it up in his mind. I say it was real because of other experiences he had. He was very much in tune with the world around him.

I was recently told by Spirit that there is a crystal cave near me and there were fairies who lived there and for me to find them because they want to communicate with me. I will look in the spring when the snow goes.

There is a whole other world to see if we would relax and look at what is before us.

PEGGY HALL FLAGG

PAST LIVES

We don't usually remember our past lifetimes because before we were born we drink from the fountain of forgetfulness or we could say, there is a veil around us. As we grow in awareness the veil becomes thinner and thinner and we can tap into past life-times.

If we clearly remembered other life-times we would be confused and not know our present reality. An example of this was a thirty five year old man I had in a group once. He was very psychic and very likable but very confused. He had passed on before and hurried to incarnate again before regrouping his last life-time and before touching with God. His past three life-times were visible to him and he didn't know the present. He was very needy and was always calling me and I had to protect myself so he didn't drain my energy. His confusion led to suicide which was a shame to waste so much. He left me his crystals for helping him as much as I could. I helped him to the light this time so he could touch with God. He was still in a hurry and reincarnated right away.

We all have the ability to tap into our past lives. Often there is a bleed through where you see yourself in another country or in a certain time frame not of now. It's interesting to know who you were or the role you played because we are the sum total of every thought we have ever thought.

I have had many lifetimes and one I will share with you is when my husband this lifetime was my husband in another. We lived in Ireland and he was a minister and I was his wife and used to go in to the fields where the peasants were working and teach them to read. The magistrate in town gave my husband a very hard time about preaching. One day I visited the magistrate and had words with him and I don't know what happened but he never bothered my husband again. Moving ahead to this lifetime, my husband has backed me in what I wanted to do.

If you are interested, there are people who can regress you and you can see for yourself who and what you experienced. I have regressed quite a few people who usually want to know about their feelings toward another person. One for example is that she didn't trust another person but didn't have a known reason this lifetime. This went back to a past lifetime when the other person betrayed her.

Another example was this woman who wanted a man and eventually marriage, but her relationships never seemed to last. As soon as she became really interested, something would happen and they would break up. In a regression it was found out that she had promised to love another man forever, not knowing forever wasn't just that lifetime but eternity. We talked with the soul and explained that this was another lifetime and the agreement was void. That ended the cycle of broken relationships for her.

As we see and feel more we become aware of the world around us and grow until we see a bigger picture and then keep evolving.

CREATION

I will leave the creation of planet Earth to be explained by the scientists. Mother Earth was created as a free will planet and to be used as a school where every level of consciousness exists. We can learn from each other when we have all levels of awareness, unlike some planets where the vibration of the souls are the same and they are there to learn a specific lesson. Mother Earth is the creative planet in the universe so while you are here, create, create!

God shines His light on all planets. God is the all. God is intelligent energy and He can be many places at once. I call God a "He" because God is male vibration like earth is female vibration. God shines his light on all of us along with the twelve main archangels.

In the bible, Revelations, chapter seven, it refers to the 144,000 souls and 12,000 each belonged to the twelve different tribes. The tribes are who we know of as the twelve archangels; Michael, Raphael, Uriel, Gabriel etc. Many of the 144,00 souls have reincarnated and are here on planet Earth to help hold the light and share with others while the planet is going through the transition of going to the fifth dimensions. The 144,000 are also known as angels. Are you one of the 144,000?

Jesus is God manifested. Jesus had many incarnations and had a high level of consciousness when he was born as Jesus. Because of his high level, God worked and shared with him so he could become a way-shower for the rest of the world. God wants us all to follow Jesus's example and basically be love. Jesus said, "This that I do he shall do also; and greater works than these shall he do."

Jesus did not come to be worshiped but for you to follow his example.

God hid the truth of the universe and the process of the soul through eternity where no one would think to look. He hid it inside each individual. So look within to find the answers.

How many of us think we can find our answers through another individual or out there somewhere? You have all you answers inside. Meditate and listen.

NEGATIVITY

One thing I realize is that God created the Earth for us to survive. For trees, plants and animals and humans to find things on the earth that help in our incarnation.

Mother Earth has gone through a lot of aches, pains, and dark times. Some of the most negative that I have heard and experienced were the wars; Civil, Revolutionary, the wars in Asia and Europe (World War II was horrendous with Nazi Germany) and many others.

All negativity goes into the ground or stays in the area. For example, When I visited Gettysburg, Pa. I could see some soldiers still fighting the war. Of course, these men hadn't realized they had transitioned. The Civil War left a huge impact on the citizens of the US as more US men were killed in that war than any other we have been involved in.

The crucifixion was another major event which was a dark time. Many think good came from it.

Mother Earth feels everything that happens on her surface.

We are destroying the planet by drilling holes in her, fracking, mining and bombing. Many of these things cause earthquakes. Hurricanes are created by negativity. A lot of hurricanes come out of the Middle East where there is much negativity. There have been so many wars in the Middle East that there is negativity in the ground. We create a lot of the weather by out thinking.

I always think it's great when the wind blows as I see it as a cleansing. The wind is blowing the pollution out of the area.

We pollute our atmosphere, we pollute our water. I worry someday that fresh clean water won't be available. We are contaminating her life blood and she is having a hard time breathing. We need to change and start loving and respecting Mother Earth to a greater degree.

If you don't recycle, it is time to. Don't litter. More needs to be done with reusable energy. The sun is a great source of energy and it's a matter of harnessing it. Tesla had great ideas about driving a rod into the ground at certain energy points--that takes some experimental processes. It seems someone who is into science can use that method to create energy if certain people don't buy the pattern or do away with the inventor.

ENERGY

Everything is energy and this energy is easy to see. A person emanates energy all around him/her. The energy is colored and denotes what a person is feeling and thinking. When you want to see the aura, begin by looking around a person's head because it is more concentrated there. If there is a white background it's much easier to see at first.

All color has a meaning so if you know what the colors mean you can discern a lot about the person. We have the color around us at all times. Sometimes you may feel the color, have an inner knowing or hear a voice, or have a thought of what the color is.

Some examples I have found are: Red; love, passion, courage. Orange; original, warm, striking. Yellow; fun, joy, optimistic. Green; nature, healing, hope. Blue; desire, relating, communication. Violet; devotion, faith, royalty. As you see the energy around a person, you will learn what the colors mean to you.

We attract other people by how we are feeling or thinking. If you attract someone undesirable than change something; thinking or feeling. We attract what we put out. If we are feeling warm and loving then we attract others who are feeling the same way.

I always use other people as a mirror because like attracts like. If you don't like what you are seeing, change your thinking.

The energy goes all around a person's body and if you can see auras you can tell where a person doesn't feel well. If there is a hole in the aura or a different shade of color in a certain area then that is where something is off or hurting in the body. For example, I saw a person once who had a dark area around her stomach and asked if she felt okay and she had been having an upset stomach and cramps. The individual sees or feels where the energy is off by different means. Some feel a difference in temperature from the rest of the body, some see lightness or darkness and some just seem to know.

Notice next time you go out in public how people respond to you. Do they smile and say something or do they act as though you are invisible? Sometimes when I go grocery shopping people go out of their way to say something or ask my opinion as to which would be the best choice between two items.

As I said, everything has energy. If you see a fly on a white ceiling notice the white light around it. Notice your cat or dog's energy. How does a room feel when you go in? If you go visiting how does the place feel? Do you feel comfortable or do you immediately want to leave?

Always compact your own energy before going somewhere. Use your own technique or at least see your self surrounded by white light. By surrounding yourself with light you are compacting your energy and protecting yourself from a lot of negativity.

In the next chapter we will explore how nature in its design can assist us in our process.

MEDICINES

As I observe people, animals and the world around me I realize God knew what he was doing. Surprise? Everything compliments and usually depends on something else. Everything has a purpose and everything is in it's place. Many times the purpose includes a combination of two or more to be effective.

Sometimes I look at the food chain and don't think it's fair but, for instance, the little fish probably have accomplished their purpose before the larger fish eats it.

Nature has been providing medicines to treat diseases and relieve our suffering for thousands of years. There have been great advances in drug design in which new medicines are synthesized but most are still derived from, or patterned after natural compounds from plants, animals and microbes.

Some compounds from plants that have been important for human medicine include morphine from the opium poppy, aspirin from the white willow tree, and the anticoagulant Coumadin from spoiled sweet clover.

Some medicine from animals, including the ACE inhibitors for treating high blood pressures come from Pit Vipers, and there is a medicine from the marine sponge used in treating AIDS.

Sea animals provide us with medicine, especially the sponge and microbes. Microbes have given us nearly all our antibiotics such as penicillin, cholesterol-lowering statins, and material that is used to coat arterial stents.

Venom from snakes, scorpions, and sea creatures can heal. It turns out that when used the right way, the poisons that would typically kill us can actually save our lives, too.

A particular protein found in spider venom, for example, could work as a treatment for muscular dystrophy. Tarantulas have been shown to have healing properties in their venom. One use is to block chronic pain by blocking the nerve activity.

In the following pages I have tried to cover some of the vibrations and healing aspects of the trees, plants and animals that God supplied us with. These properties are intended to be used for our own good.

TREES

Planet Earth provides healing and food through nature and has since the beginning. For centuries man has made healing medicine from nature going back to the Native Americans and way before.

I married into a lumberman family and they logged and sawed. I could identify most trees by the leaves and bark. My husband could identify the boards after they were sawed. Trees of all kinds provide many uses not to mention the beauty of each.

I know 700 years ago my mother then was known as 'Medicine Woman'. Many came to her for her remedies from plants and herbs that grew wild. We were on the West coast in Southern California. One thing she made was a tea from the redwood tree. It has several healing capabilities and probably best known for helping lung issues. One cup was enough because it is so potent.

Redwood

The redwood is a symbol of forever, a great teacher of ancient wisdom. Redwoods are the tallest trees on earth. They really have a birds eye view of the world. The key to the survival is the ability to regenerate.

Oak

Bravery, strength and magnificence is the vibration of the sturdy oak, which represents the tree of life. The oak serves as food for squirrels and other animals.

It is said the oak tree drives away fear, is good for the emotions, eases blood problems, kidney stones and improves circulation. The oak makes beautiful furniture for home and office. When I was in the antique business a few years ago, everyone wanted a round oak table and matching chairs. I could have sold at least one a week.

Pine

The pine tree has many uses. I can remember my grandmother steeping pine needles and adding honey to make cough syrup. That was my cure-all for cold related issues from chest congestion to a sore throat. The pine tree drives away all harm to the home, family and especially to new born infants; heals the chest, throat and lung infections. They are beautiful year round as they keep their green needles and are never bare although they shed needles and grow new ones.

Resin from pine trees as well as other conifers has many uses. The pitch is boiled down to a solid and sometimes chemicals are added. Resin (in the form of rosin) is also used on musical instruments. If you have been involved in some sports, I'm sure you had the use of a rosin bag to rub your hands around to make them sticky so the ball wouldn't slip so easily.

The pine tree provides many uses from medicine to wood for furniture and boards for building with the knots showing not to mention the stately beauty of each tree.

Hemlock

The hemlock is another conifer that provides food for the deer during winter months. The tree is always trimmed of branches as high as the deer can reach. This is their basic food during snow season.

Cedar

Cedar trees symbolize healing, cleansing and protection. They are considered purifying by Native Americans. Spiritual people usually have cedar and sage in their house and smudge the house often to help keep it cleansed. Some people have cedar chests of all sizes to store objects in for keepsakes and anything the want to smell good.

Ash

The ash tree symbolizes how inner and outer worlds are linked. They represent sensitivity and higher awareness. The wood is strong and called hardwood. It is also elastic. The wood is used for baseball bats, handles for tools, as well as bowls and some furniture.

Birch

Birch trees bring new beginnings, protect mothers and their young; help reduce fluid retention, high cholesterol levels, and skin issues. Birch trees will sometimes have a certain kind of mushroom growing on them. There seems to be many uses for tinctures made from this mushroom. The extracts are said to be beneficial for different cancers,  high blood pressure, diabetes, cholesterol and good for the immune system.

Apple

Remember the saying "An apple a day keeps the doctor away"? It is said that the apple is very healing in many ways and particularly it helps heal the inner organs and digestive tract. The apple tree brings fertility, self-love and gradually restores health and optimism.

We cook apples in many ways from apple pie, cakes and many desserts plus I grate a small one into a meat loaf. The use of an apple is endless including apple cider and vinegar. Vinegar is useful in food preparation especially used in salad dressings and taken in a little water for balancing the PH in a person's body that is too acidic. I know of some people that took vinegar and honey everyday as a medicine. Elderly folks took these home remedies to maintain their health.

Note: I have two McIntosh apple trees in my back yard and two Bartlett pear trees. The trees look very healthy and green each year and never produce any fruit. I couldn't understand why. This year I heard that two different kinds of the trees are needed to cross pollinate. So I need to purchase another kind of apple tree and another kind of pear tree.

I should have learned this from my childhood as we had many kinds of fruit trees on the farm but they were planted many years before I was born.

Cherry

The cherry tree symbolizes renewal, rejuvenation and new beginnings. It is also called the tree of the heart because of the energy it has in helping a person find the true self. It is also called the friendship tree because of the gift to the US from Japan. What is more beautiful then the cherry trees in bloom in Washington DC?

Of course, the fruit is delicious.

All fruit trees provide many vitamins that help boost our immune system to help fight viruses.

I always have tea tree oil in the house. This comes from the melaleuca tree which is native to Australia but is now found in other places including Southern Florida. This is a my favorite on the physical body for blisters, burns, fungus, arthritis, athletes food, used in a vaporizer for bronchial infections and on and on and on. Tea tree oil is also good as a household cleaner. I understand a honey can be made of it to treat wounds.

There is no end to the healing aids made from trees that also provide shade, food for some animals and nest for birds. Trees are also emotionally healing if you lean against one or walk in the woods.

PLANTS

Plants are the most valuable part of nature as far as making medicinal cures.

A lot of people in this area are herbalists and classes are abundant where one can learn about the plants and how to use them as medicinal remedies. Many old remedies are handed down from earlier generations when a pharmacy was not available.

We had a homeopathic doctor who delivered me when I was born and was my doctor up until he retired when I was 28. He also delivered two of my children. When I went to him he would pull out about 3 or 4 different bottles and use so much of each one but never measured anything. What a memory he had. Back then he never took notes on anything but remembered everything. That was back when he made house calls and when he came to our house, when I was young, he always planned to sit down and have a piece of pie and coffee. My mother always had pie in the house and when she knew he was coming she baked some of his favorites.

The plants that are beneficial to us are too numerous to name but some of the most common I have listed below (I am talking about the plants of the North Eastern US).

Dandelion

Dandelion symbolizes perseverance and represents tenaciousness. It is prevalent and nearly everywhere in the Northern Hemisphere. It is a plant that won't give up finding a spot to grow. Many times we call dandelion a nuisance especially on our lawns.

The common dandelion is very abundant and can serve many purposes. We used to dig them and gather the fresh greens and boil them, and sometimes my mother would add salt pork to the process. I like them and always used vinegar on them.

The dandelion is entirely edible and has beta carotene and a great amount of iron.

Dandelion is a good remedy for many things: It is a good diuretic, preventative for kidney stones, to lower high blood pressure, for skin problems and helps with diabetes. An herbalist makes a tincture or tea for different purposes.

Plantain

Plantain is another healing "weed". It has the vibration of healing, relaxation and adaptability. Much like the dandelion it has many medicinal uses. Edgar Cayce, the sleeping prophet, mentions plantain many times in his readings for healing purposes.

Plantain may vary in size. It is very common, growing on the lawn, in the field, beside the road and can get large if there is moisture. `Plantain is basically an astringent. It is good for stings and bug bites. A tea made from plantain is good for respiratory conditions. The whole plant can be used and made into salve (liquid, butter-like or jelly) for different ailments.

Mullien

Mullein is another common plant /weed. It seems to be flexible and nurturing.

Mullein isn't particular where it grows and can be found along the road side and places where other plants refuse to grow. This too is helpful to the respiratory conditions. It can aid in bladder control and is beneficial as a cough remedy. It is also helpful in killing certain bacteria.

Burdock

Burdock gives off the vibration of a loner. It isn't a welcoming plant and thrives by itself.

Most of us call burdock a nuisance because the burrs cling to everything that it touches and are prickly and hard to remove, especially from dog fur. It is known as a blood purifier and a diuretic. It can also aid in digestion. The root is dried and ground into powder for use in a tea or a tincture.

The Native Americans had many uses for Burdock including pleurisy and coughs. Somehow it was used in their ceremonies.

Jewelweed

Jewelweed is a pretty plant with the blossoms of orange with darker red spots. It gives out the vibration of being independent and represents purity.

Jewelweed is also known as "touch-me-not" because it's made of a soft flaky tissue that tends to expel it's contents if touched or shaken. It is used in the treatment of poison ivy, rheumatism, bruises and swelling. It is good for any skin irritants.

This is well liked by deer as it tastes good to them and maybe it has a healing effect.

Fern

Ferns symbolize magic, fascination, confidence and is associated with the spiritual realms.

Sweet fern grows in fields and along the road side. It is used to relieve itching and skin conditions that are irritating. It is used for all kinds of rashes. My grandmother thought it was wonderful for poison ivy. The ferns would be steeped and the liquid used to bathe the body. It can be used for indigestion and stomach cramps. A tea may be made to aid these issues.

Daisy

Daisy is a representative of innocence, simplicity and purity. Teas and infusions may be made from daisies for healing (but I don't usually think of a daisy as a healing plant because of it's beauty prettiness in a bouquet). They have cleansing properties, are good as mild laxatives and will increase the appetite. The teas can promote sweating to reduce fever, fight infections and treat respiratory issues.

Elderberry

I think the Elderberry bush gives off a vibration of protection and love for all who use the berries.

The elderberry bush usually grows in moist areas or even beside the road. The blossoms are picked by the cluster and dried and then a tea may be made. It is used when there is a cold and /or flu when one has a temperature. This helps bring the temperature down. Elderberries may also be used in making wine. I have never made wine but some people like it.

At one time I had a large elderberry bush behind my house and when I thought the bush was ready I called my friend, who is an herbalist, and she would harvest them. I have no idea where the bush came from but credit the birds for dropping there.

Blackberry

Blackberry's medicinal property is a strong astringency. All parts of the bush may be used. It is used as a remedy for diarrhea and is also helpful if one has a sore throat. Blackberry tea is quite tasteful.

I want to include a couple of plants that don't grow wild in nature.

Sunflowers

Sunflowers are associated with adoration and spiritualism. Sunflowers turn their heads to the sun as Spiritualists turn toward the Light of the Divine. Sunflowers represents life as they have 7 branches, (7 days in a week) 12 leaves, (12 months in a year), 52 yellow petals (52 weeks in a year) and each flower has 365 seeds (365 days in a year). Start counting.

Hosta

I don't know of any medicinal use for hosta but the deer really love the foliage. They keep my hosta in the landscaping in front of my house well eaten. They will eat it down to ground level and when it grows back they seem to know and visit again. I replaced my rhododendron twice and gave up and selected some prickly evergreens to keep the deer from eating my plants.

--

I want to share this as it may help someone out there who has the same issue:

Ever since I had surgery three years ago I have been short of breath. Spirit said I had fluid in the bottom of my lungs and to have kale twice a day. I don't particularity like kale as a salad but mixed in a shake it's pretty good. At this point it has been about three weeks and I'm still on kale. Because I know all the other benefits I will continue for awhile and then maybe have it once a day. The kale works as an expectorant for me and I do breathe better.

I could go one and on as many more plants are used for medicinal remedies. Especially fruit trees, berries and the plants we call weeds.

Plants are part of the food chain not only for human use but for the birds and animals. I need to get out and pick the blueberries on my property before the birds eat them all!

PEGGY HALL FLAGG

ANIMALS

Medicine is everything that improves one's connection to the Great Mystery of life. This can include healing of the body, mind, and spirit. It's anything that brings personal power, strength and understanding.

Animals exhibit patterns that will relay messages of healing to anyone aware enough to observe their lessons on how to live. Each lesson is based on one major concept and each animal has been assigned one of these lessons.

Each and every person has power animals that represent the medicine in their Earth Walk. For instance the owl. The owl is associated with clairvoyance, astral projection, and magic. This means if an owl is one of your power animals you can draw on him for the understanding and healing of his essence.

The Native Americans worked with the concepts of their power animals. These animals and their vibrations are very important to them.

Years ago before we had farms and raised cattle people depended on wild animals for their survival. I am talking of the Native Americans who killed buffalo, deer, elk and other animals for their food plus used the hides for clothing. Every part of the animal was used.

Some other examples:

Moose

Wisdom and self-esteem is the vibration of the moose. Especially the male moose as he has great pride in his maleness and thinks all the ladies want his seed.

The bones of moose were use to make different tools like awls, spears, fish hooks, and harpoons. The antlers were used sometimes as a digging device and the fat was rubbed on children's skin for various illnesses. There was never any waste and much of the moose was made into soup.

Beaver

The beaver is the doer in the animal kingdom. He takes great pride in his family and home. In his dam are many entrances and exits for escape routes. He's smart because he is not going to paint himself into a corner.

Beaver was used for medicinal purposes as well as food. Some of the larger skins were used as saddle blankets and made into winter clothing as well.

The teeth were often made into necklaces. Beaver teeth were sometimes ground into powder and added to soup to help children with colds and congestion.

The pelts were traded for other needs and sometimes for supplemental income. Beavers are still trapped today. The beavers, at times, have caused floods by the trees they have downed. Think what they must have for teeth!

Deer

Deer symbolize gentleness, sensitivity and innocence. The Native Americans believed deer could provide knowledge of the pharmacology of plants (I don't always think they are so innocent when I catch them eating my landscaping in front of the house).

If the deer is one of your power animals you are asked to be gentle in spirit to heal all wounds. They ask you to stop pushing others to change but to love them as they are.

Some societies think the deer antler is powerful in healing, circulation, kidney function, and weakness of the back and legs. The antler is ground into powder and sometimes added to tortoise shell because of its richness in gelatin.

Of course, most of us know what deer meat tastes like and venison is considered a delicacy in many areas and restaurants. Many different foods can be made from deer meat.

The skin makes nice soft slippers and gloves and many other items. Many products are made from the complete deer.

Snake

The power of the snake is the power of creation, psychic energy, reproduction, sexuality and ascension.

There are healing properties of rattlesnakes and that is the snake oil that is used in massage, to cure baldness (I should have recommended that to my husband) and as a chest rub for congestion.

Years ago, salesmen traveled to different places selling snake oil. Sometimes it would contain rattle snake fat and some times the elixir would have nothing but alcohol and water. Snake oil has a negative connotation because the salesmen tried to sell their cure-all which was merely alcohol and no snake oil. The customer probably felt better for a few hours.

Parts of the snake is used in Mexico for various remedies. Mixed with other things it is thought to calm the nerves, help arthritis, kidney problems and cancer.

If the snake is your power animal there is a need to transmute some thought, action or desire so wholeness can be achieved. This is a heavy magic, but remember, magic is no more than a change of consciousness.

Most wild animals provide healing properties of some kind. Instinctively they know how to heal themselves, many times by licking their wounds. Even domestic animals have healing powers. The dog's saliva contains a protein that promotes healing to the dog himself and people if they allow licking of their wound. Dogs symbolize unconditional love and protection.

Cats symbolize independence, mystery, magic and cleverness (and of course curiosity). The cats purring vibration is said to speed the healing of bones. Sound waves are used today in certain healings of the body. I think we are going to hear more and more about healing with sound.

It has been found that infants who have a pet in their environment for the first six months of their life are less likely to develop allergies and asthma and are less likely to have colds and ear infections during their first year.

If you are a meditator you can ask Spirit to give you the different power animals you have around you. Or you could go to a person who does readings and they can tell you.

God made everything on earth to help all things survive.

NEXT STEP

Everyone has their own evolutionary path according to an individual choice. The next step for some is another dimension which will be the 5th. The evolutionary paths could be creator path, teacher path, healer path or human path.

We are in the 3rd dimension here on planet earth and when we are preparing to go to the 5th, we are in the 4th for a short period of time while making the transition. To qualify, a person's vibration needs to vibrate at the same speed as the 5th dimension.

There are many dimensions right here but because we vibrate at a different speed we don't see those in another dimension, so the only change there is that those around you will all be vibrating at the same speed. Things will be different because you have graduated to a higher level.

The new earth will look much like this earth. It will have trees like ours but no redwoods as they have completed their evolution. There will be a collage of flowers and plants.

The animals will be much more limited, we will have a type of dog, a type of cat, koala bears and elephants. The elephants here in the 3 rd hold the energy for the planet and also do some work for God.

There will be a variety of fish but no sharks. There will be whales and dolphins but they are from another star system. Star fish also, they are from the 3rd star system.

The only insect will be the beetles. The fairies will go back to pollinating flowers, trees and anything that needs pollinating. In the beginning God assigned the fairies that job but the bees came along and frightened them away. I wonder if that is the reason the bees are disappearing?

I don't see any predatory animals or birds, this a planet of peace.

There will be advanced technology, cars will be way beyond our current imagination and we will program in our destination and arrive there. Maybe this is where our GPS idea came from. The cars will be merkabas and everyone who wants will learn to drive.

There will be no money, we will create things. Or if we want a pair of shoes we will go to a store and order them and they will be delivered the next day. People create different things.

There won't be doctors as we know them but energy workers. There will be healers who work with a persons inner world, a healer who works with external, a healer who works with the mind and brain. There will also be healers who work with vision, not the eyes directly but the third eye. A psychic surgeon, who works outside the body like a neurosurgeon, and a tooth doctor The placement of teeth will be different.

There won't be any invasive surgery because everything will be done energetically. There will be people like nurses who will hold your hand if needed.

No vaccinations.

No need for insurance.

We won't have computers but a monitor in each home.

If you want a new career, there will be education to learn. It may be something you have a passion for.

As I understand it there will be no marriage but commitments. You will need to have someone of the same vibration and on the same page. One can reproduce if they care to.

There will be less water and more land then we have now. We can desalinate water very easily but there will be fresh water lakes.

When we go to the 5th we will completely disappear and whatever belongs to us will disappear as well. We will be erased from the memory of all who knew us like we never existed. Also those that were with us in the third dimension we won't remember either.

It's 1000 years of peace and joy.

LIFE ON EARTH

The following chapter was written by my Granddaughter, Hannah.

Her college course in environmental studies took her to different parts of the US where she experienced many different environments and survival techniques of the area. I think her favorite part was time spent on the waterways.

Hannah shares some of the places she most enjoyed.

Thanks Hannah for sharing with us.

PEGGY HALL FLAGG

THE RUGGED LANDSCAPES THAT WE CALL HOME
By: Hannah Flagg

The vast rugged landscapes that one calls home, whether for a period of a lifetime or simply a few weeks while traveling through, can shape an individual. The deserts, the mountains, and the river valleys around the world all have unique characteristics that allow them to survive in the environments that encompass them. There is no one place that is similar to another; each one has different terrains, climates, and people who travel through it. People who are breathing and seeing the wildness that is surrounding them. These landscapes can inspire people and communities, which ultimately can foster change in how people interact with the land. By living and traveling to different places, individuals can gain a greater connection to the land, have a greater sense of place, and gain a higher level of wanting to protect the places one calls home.

I have been fortunate enough in my twenty-four years of life so far on Earth to visit unique wild landscapes in different corners of the hemisphere. From Maine to the watersheds of the South West corner of the United States, all the way to Alaska, these places have changed me and allowed me to see the world through a different set of eyes. The Yukon River, the Sea of Cortez, and the Grand Canyon are three different landscapes that I am going to share.

The Yukon River in Alaska is a mighty river that travels about two thousand miles to the Bering Sea from British Columbia. It sustains villages and people who live next to it during the harsh winter months, by allowing communities to harvest salmon during the warmer months to provide nourishment to their families. It provided transportation during the Klondike Gold Rush and now is home to a few remanding communities such as the people of Fort Yukon, which is above the Arctic Circle. While traveling 500 miles through this landscape, the question that kept coming up in my head was: what would this place be like if it had a larger human impact?

The Yukon River, Alaska Photo: Hannah Flagg

The Sea of Cortez in Mexico is unique in which there are cacti and whales all in one view. The sacred island of Isle de Tiberon is filled with wonder and awe. The marine life is spectacular and inspiring; one can view dolphins swimming four feet from one's own sea kayak. The saltwater is as warm as the sea breeze. What are the impacts on the ecosystems from fisheries? Are their large human impacts here by surrounding communities?

The Sea of Cortez, Mexico Photo: Hannah Flagg

The Grand Canyon of the Colorado River is home to deep canyon walls and raging whitewater. During the day it can be a scorching one hundred degrees, while the river is still 45 degrees. Flash floods can take over kitchens while at camp during down pours and crazy thunderstorms. A lot of questions come up on this river; what would this landscape look like without dams? What is the price we pay for commercial motor craft to travel through this rugged beautiful landscape?

The Grand Canyon Photo: Hannah Flagg

No matter what questions related to human impact go through my head while exploring these landscapes, I believe at the root of it all we need to protect it in whatever capacity we can. There are many ways that individuals and groups of people can protect the land and water for generations to come. Whether at a national, state or individual level, change needs to occur not just for the planet but to sustain people's happiness, wellbeing, and inspiration.

Standing up and protecting the sacred land that is at risk to development, over-forestation, or drilling is not the only thing we can do. As a community we can look at sustainable fishing practices whether in our home state or in Alaska to feed and sustain communities for generations to come. We can look at water quality within wastewater dumping and how it is impacting other resources. Every avenue that a community can look down can in fact impact and protect the landscapes for future generations. Living simply, doesn't have to mean living off the land, but living off the land can be achieved.

And as for one of my mottoes of life; "make the indoor space as livable as the outdoor space, and make the outdoor space livable as the indoor". With that, I think one will be able to sustain and protect the planet no matter where they are and make the place where they are traveling through, living, or dreaming about, home.

ABOUT THE AUTHOR

Peggy's passion is sharing spiritual knowledge with others. Her life has been presenting lectures, leading groups and teaching classes to those just awakening. It gives her much joy to see people grow, answer their own questions and find their empowerment. This has taken Peggy to many states and some other countries for classes and also teaching.

Peggy can be reached by email at brlight@roadrunner.com.

www.ingramcontent.com/pod-product-compliance
Lightning Source LLC
Chambersburg PA
CBHW071801040426
42446CB00012B/2661